5099

NF

£2.25
UK only

D0259075

Right: Liverpool's Ray Clemence saves from the lunging boot of Manchester City's Roger Palmer.

Right: Clive Allen looks a little bewildered on his debut for Crystal Palace. Perhaps he was wondering who he was playing for.

ISBN 361 05091 7
Copyright © 1981 Purnell and Sons Limited
Published 1981 by Purnell Books, Paulton,
Bristol BS18 5LQ
Filmset in Great Britain by
Hazell Watson & Viney Ltd, Aylesbury, Bucks
Printed and bound by Purnell and Sons Ltd.,
Paulton (Bristol) and London.

Football Champions

Edited by Norman Barrett

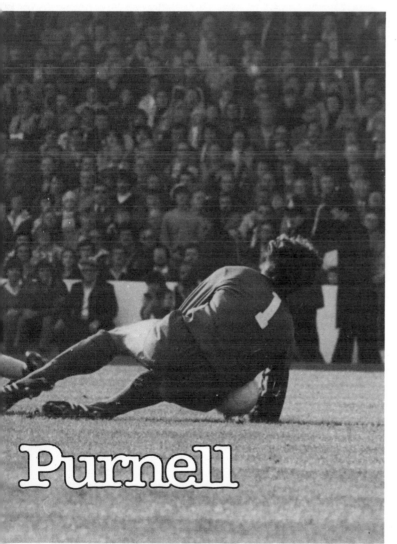

Purnell

Southampton's Charlie George
seems upset about something.

Above: Aston Villa celebrate their first League Championship for 71 years. Thousands of fans thronged to Birmingham Town Hall as manager Ron Saunders (left) and captain Dennis Mortimer display the trophy. Left: Dutch star Frans Thijssen, the midfield inspiration of Ipswich in a marvellous season that saw them win the UEFA Cup, was voted Footballer of the Year. Below: Leading scorers — Peter Withe of Villa (left) and Steve Archibald of Spurs led Division 1 with 20 League goals apiece, while Celtic's Frank McGarvey (inset) was leading Premier Division scorer in Scotland with 23.

Honours of the 1980~81 Season

Football League Champions	**ASTON VILLA**
Runners-up	Ipswich Town
FA Cup Winners	**TOTTENHAM HOTSPUR**
Runners-up	Manchester City
League Cup Winners	**LIVERPOOL**
Runners-up	West Ham United
Division Two Champions	**WEST HAM UNITED**
Runners-up	Notts County
Also promoted	Swansea City
Division Three Champions	**ROTHERHAM UNITED**
Runners-up	Barnsley
Also promoted	Charlton Athletic
Division Four Champions	**SOUTHEND UNITED**
Runners-up	Lincoln City
Also promoted	Doncaster Rovers and Wimbledon
Scottish Premier Division Champions	**CELTIC**
Runners-up	Aberdeen
Scottish Cup Winners	**RANGERS**
Runners-up	Dundee United
Scottish League Cup Winners	**DUNDEE UNITED**
Runners-up	Dundee
Scottish Division One Champions	**HIBERNIAN**
Runners-up	Dundee
Scottish Division Two Champions	**QUEEN'S PARK**
Runners-up	Queen of the South
Footballer of the Year	**FRANS THIJSSEN** (Ipswich)
Players' Player of the Year	**JOHN WARK** (Ipswich)
Young Player of the Year	**GARY SHAW** (Aston Villa)
Scottish Player of the Year	**ALAN ROUGH** (Partick)
Scottish Young Player of the Year	**CHARLIE NICHOLAS** (Celtic)
European Cup Winners	**LIVERPOOL** (England)
Runners-up	Real Madrid (Spain)
European Cup-Winners' Cup Winners	**DYNAMO TBLISI** (USSR)
Runners-up	Carl Zeiss Jena (East Germany)
UEFA Cup Winners	**IPSWICH TOWN** (England)
Runners-up	AZ 67 Alkmaar (Netherlands)

Above: Ricardo Villa, Spurs' wayward Argentinian star, proudly holds the FA Cup aloft. Taken off at Wembley almost in tears after a lack-lustre display, he roared back in the replay with a glorious winning goal. **Below:** Phil Thompson 'wears' the League Cup, the first time Liverpool had won this trophy. During a season in which they were overshadowed for much of the time by Aston Villa and Ipswich, they won the European Cup, too.

The FA Cup

Round by Round Highlights

Third Round

Mick Lyons (above) leaves Pat Jennings helpless as he scores Everton's second, and celebrates (right), with a disconsolate David O'Leary behind him.

Only three non-League clubs made it to the Third Round this year, and two of these were dispatched promptly. Altrincham had to face the Kop at Anfield, and their 4-1 defeat was no disgrace. Maidstone succumbed 4-2 at home to Exeter, and in view of the Third Division side's later exploits in the tournament, neither was theirs. The only non-Leaguers to win through were Isthmians Enfield, who held Port Vale away and demolished them 3-0 in the replay.

Last year's finalists West Ham and Arsenal were both knocked out. For Arsenal, it meant that their Wembley run had come to an end — they had appeared in the last three finals. They held Everton at Goodison for 85 minutes before Kenny Sansom diverted a cross into his own goal, and then substitute Mick Lyons made it 2-0 in the last minute.

Cup-holders West Ham lasted a little longer before they gave up their crown. With a record of 17 consecutive home wins behind them, their tie against Wrexham seemed a formality. But nothing can ever be taken for granted in the Cup. West Ham were leading 1-0 with only 3 minutes to go, when Wrexham central defender Gareth Davis forced the ball home from close range. Ironically, he had moved upfield only because he thought Wrexham had won a corner, when in fact it was a throw-in! The two sides fought out a goalless draw in the replay three days later, and after a postponement it was another two weeks before an extra-time goal by Dixie McNeil settled the issue in the second replay, at Wrexham.

Two big clubs had frights at home before scraping a draw. Forest were twice behind to Bolton before Raimondo Ponte made it 3-3 with only six minutes to go. And Manchester United were two down at half-time to Brighton. Both Forest and United won their replays, although it took an extra-time goal by Trevor Francis to rescue Forest from a further replay.

An intriguing tie took place at Maine Road, where Manchester City entertained Crystal Palace. The special interest this match generated was due to the return of recently sacked City manager Malcolm Allison, who was now in charge of the struggling Palace. Meanwhile, under John Bond, City had been enjoying a revival, and they continued in the same vein by brushing Palace aside 4-0.

The 'crunch' match of the Third Round was Ipswich v Aston Villa, with both clubs currently disputing First Division leadership with Liverpool. The match was no classic, however, Ipswich winning with a 14th-minute Mariner goal after superb work by Thijssen.

The highest score, and perhaps the finest performance, of the round belonged to Middlesbrough. They won 5-0 away to Swansea City, themselves at that time standing second in Division II. Considering Middlesbrough's dismal away record in the League — two wins, nine losses, and only nine goals in the 11 matches they had played — this was an extraordinary result . . . but quite in keeping with the unpredictability of the Cup.

Below: Alan Brazil of Ipswich (left) goes for the ball while Villa's Allan Evans looks on.

Above: Phil Boyer (left) nips in to beat the Palace keeper for Manchester City's third goal.

Fourth Round

The non-League challenge ended in this round, but not before Enfield had shocked Barnsley on their own ground with a last-minute equaliser. They allowed the return to be held at Spurs, and over 35,000 turned up at White Hart Lane to see their dreams shattered by Barnsley's 3-0 victory.

Enfield, however, outlasted Liverpool, who went out of the Cup 2-1 to rivals Everton at Goodison. For so long embarrassed by the success of their neighbours, Everton fought fiercely in this aggressive local derby, in which three players from each side were booked. It was a rare victory for the 'Toffeemen' over the League Champions.

Another clash of First Division giants took place at the City Ground, where Nottingham Forest entertained Manchester United, and beat them with a Trevor Francis goal. But it was more, perhaps, to the saves of Peter Shilton and the defensive heroics of Kenny Burns that Forest owed their victory. Shilton produced two miraculous saves to thwart Gary Birtles, who was making his first return to Forest since his £1·2 million transfer 10 weeks previously.

Again interest centred on Manchester City's home tie. Manager John Bond had come to them, somewhat controversially, from opponents Norwich earlier in the season, and his son Kevin was still playing for Norwich. City showed Norwich no mercy, however, and beat them 6-0, but they lost striker Phil Boyer for the rest of the season through injury.

Despite Leicester's position at the foot of the First Division table, it was a surprise when Exeter held them to a draw at Filbert Street. The replay produced probably the finest individual performance of the round — a hat-trick from Exeter striker Tony Kellow, which gave them a 3-1 victory.

Gary Birtles (right), returned to Forest for the first time since his transfer to Manchester.

Fifth Round

Seven First Division sides triumphed in the eight Fifth Round matches, the only other victors being giant-killers Exeter of the Third. They earned a replay with a late equaliser at St James' Park – Newcastle's home – and produced a scintillating display at their own St James' Park to thrash the Second Division side 4-0.

Everton beat their third Division I opponents. They held the fancied Southampton to a goalless draw at The Dell, spoiling Kevin Keegan's 30th birthday, and a brilliant extra-time goal by Eamonn O'Keefe broke the deadlock in the replay.

Nottingham Forest, exhausted by their midweek trip to Tokyo for the World Club Championship and perhaps disheartened at losing, almost suffered the shock of the round. They were a goal down at home to Bristol City (languishing near the bottom of Division II and without an away win all season), when John Robertson equalised from the penalty spot seven minutes from the end. Five minutes later, Ian Wallace put them through.

Manchester City went marching on, although their 1-0 victory at Peterborough was the least convincing of their performances so far. Nor were Ipswich as dominant as expected at home to Charlton. A fine display by keeper Nicky Johns and a plethora of missed chances kept the score down to 2-0.

Spurs chalked up a confident 3-1 win over Coventry at White Hart Lane, but Wolves' defeat of Wrexham by the same score was never on the cards until they brought on their 'super sub' Norman Bell. Coming on in the second half with Wolves a goal down, he scored two swashbuckling goals in as many minutes, and John Richards added a third.

Above: Everton's Trevor Ross hurdles Nick Holmes of Southampton.

Below: Spurs' Chris Houghton (right) converts a Glenn Hoddle pass to eliminate Coventry.

Sixth Round

After the Saturday games, only Spurs had won through to the semi-finals. They beat Exeter 2-0, while the other three matches were drawn.

Even with home advantage, it took Spurs over an hour to break down the Exeter defence. And then it was only after the Third Division giant-killers had been disrupted by the loss of Ian Pearson. Graham Roberts, with his first goal for Spurs, and Paul Miller were the unlikely goal-scorers, both owing their success to Glenn Hoddle's deceptive, curling crosses.

The Forest-Ipswich match was generally acclaimed as a classic tie, worthy of a final. But one man who will want to forget it was Forest's England right-back Viv Anderson. He had a nightmare match. First, he gifted Paul Mariner a goal with a careless pass back intended for Shilton. Then he headed past his bewildered goalkeeper to give Ipswich a 2-0 lead. Finally, he dislocated his shoulder in a clash with Ipswich keeper Cooper as he went for goal. But by then Forest had clawed their way back to go in level at half time, with goals from Trevor Francis and Colin Walsh. In the second half, John Robertson gave them the lead with a penalty, and Frans Thijssen was grateful to grab a late equaliser when his shot was deflected past Shilton.

It was Thijssen who settled Ipswich down in the replay after Forest had taken charge in the first half, and it was his fellow Dutchman

As Wembley gets closer, the tensions mount, and the joy of goalscoring becomes greater. Below: Gerry Gow (centre) is congratulated by team-mates after scoring the equaliser for Manchester City only two minutes after Everton had gone ahead. Above: Frans Thijssen exhibits both joy and relief after equalising against Forest and earning Ipswich a replay.

Arnold Muhren who cracked in the only goal of the game, a great 16-yard right-foot volley after Thijssen had set up the move.

Middlesbrough lost the chance to reach their first-ever semi-final when they could only draw at home. Wolves took the replay 3-1, although they needed extra time, and it was substitute Bell again who clinched it for them with the third goal.

Everton were the third side to give up their home advantage, when they twice lost the lead against Manchester City. In an equally fierce replay on a muddy Maine Road pitch, full-back Bobby McDonald broke the goalless deadlock with two in as many minutes half-way through the second period, and City ran out 3-1 winners.

> Arnold Muhren, after putting Ipswich into the semi-finals with a right-foot volley: 'The only time I use my right foot is in the car.'

The Semi-Finals

In an attempt to avert a repeat of last year's marathon semi-final between Arsenal and Liverpool, the FA decided that extra time would be played in 1981 if necessary. It was – in both matches. And even then, one went to a replay, in extremely controversial circumstances. With Spurs leading Wolves 2-1 at Hillsborough and only a minute to go, Kenny Hibbitt went sprawling in Spurs' penalty area. Referee Clive Thomas pointed to the spot, and Willie Carr stepped up to slot in the equaliser.

Poor Thomas. Only a month earlier he had been the centre of controversy for giving Liverpool an 'offside' goal in the League Cup final. Now he was again being branded as the villain of the piece, this time together with Hibbitt, who was accused of cheating by 'taking a dive'. Not many referees would have had the courage to give a penalty in such circumstances. But TV replays suggested he was mistaken, for Glenn Hoddle, who had challenged Hibbitt, had successfully pushed the ball away. Hibbitt might have fallen over Hoddle's leg (and made a 'meal' of his fall, knowing it was Wolves' last chance), but there was no question of a foul.

There was no further score in extra time, so the match was replayed at Highbury, only a few miles from Tottenham's White Hart Lane. With this advantage and in the absence of Wolves striker Andy Gray, Spurs made no mistake.

They put on a superb performance for their fans, brushing Wolves aside 3-0. Hoddle brilliantly made two for Garth Crooks in the first half, and Ricky Villa scored a gem of a solo goal in the second.

Waiting for them were Manchester City, who had finally extinguished the Ipswich flame with a goal by captain Paul Power in the first period of extra time. Poor Ipswich — beset with injuries as the season progressed and overburdened with fixtures in their bid to bring off the treble of League, Cup, and UEFA Cup — nothing went right for them. Yet they had enough early chances to bury City, before Tommy Caton and Nicky Reid took a hold on their strikers. Kevin Beattie, making frequent sorties from the back, was desperately unlucky with three headers. Rising to an early corner, he powered the ball past the keeper but Tommy Hutchison cleared it from the line. In the second half he was just wide with a far-post header from a free-kick, and

then beat the City defence again with a diving header, only to see it bounce over the bar! Soon after that, he broke his arm in a collision, and that, sadly, was the end of Beattie's season.

Power broke the deadlock after 100 minutes. City won a disputed free-kick nearly 30 yards out. Steve Mackenzie tapped it to his captain, who sent a dipping, swerving left-foot shot past the despairing Cooper. There would be no League and Cup double in 1981.

Matchwinners. Right: Paul Power, Manchester City's goalscorer. Below: Crooks (11) and Hoddle (10), scorer and maker of Spurs' first two, chase Villa after he had clinched the replay with a superb third.

The Year of the Cockerel

Spurs win the 100th Cup final in a classic replay

Manager John Bond had worked miracles to get Manchester City to Wembley, taking them over as a bottom-of-the-table side who had lost all confidence in themselves. They had beaten four First Division teams on the way, had moved up to a comfortable mid-table position in the League, and had reached the semi-finals of the League Cup.

Nevertheless, Spurs were marginal favourites. After all, it was the 'Year of the Cockerel' according to the Chinese, and anyway Spurs were 'due' for a win in 1981, having won the Cup in 1901, 1921, and 1961 (there was no competition in 1941 because of the war). For those who believed in omens, the Cup was already on Spurs' sideboard. But more important, manager Keith Burkinshaw's perseverance with an attacking brand of football was beginning to pay dividends. Admittedly, Spurs had avoided all the 'big guns' on their path to Wembley, and their suspect defence had been strengthened more by luck than by judgement when Burkinshaw was forced to reorganise it because of injuries. But their star players — Hoddle, Ardiles, Crooks, and Archi-

bald — were consistently producing some of the most entertaining football in the country. And, as it eventually transpired, Villa was capable of reaching the heights, too.

The final was a clash of two contrasting styles of play. City's aim was to deny the Spurs midfield time to dwell on the ball, applying pressure as soon as a Spurs player got possession. They attacked largely with long balls to their strikers, Bennett and Reeves, and overlapping runs from their supporting full-backs, Ransom and McDonald. Gerry Gow was the midfield hard man, whose tackling won periods of supremacy for City but was eventually to be their undoing. Spurs, on the other hand, relied on a gradual build-up from their midfield, the subtle prising open of the opposing defence for the rapier-like thrusts of the two front men Crooks and Archibald.

Spurs kicked off in the 100th FA Cup final, but it was City who were first to threaten, forcing four corners in the first five minutes. They never allowed Spurs to settle in the first half, and on the half-hour Hutchison put City ahead, powering in a header from all of 14 yards to convert a Ransom cross after good work by Bennett and Reeves.

Yet despite the City pressure, this was the first time Aleksic had been seriously threatened. Joe Corrigan, on the other hand, was forced to produce three first-class saves — from Roberts, Galvin, and Crooks. Graham Roberts, who had been playing non-League football only a year earlier, was outstanding in Spurs' defence. But he took a fearful kick in the face from team-mate Chris Houghton near half-time, which left him streaming with blood and minus a tooth. Fortunately for Spurs, he was able to play on, and it did not appear to affect his play.

Corrigan comes out to deny Crooks an early equaliser.

Half-way through the second half, Spurs brought on young Gary Brooke for the ineffective Villa. His enthusiasm made an immediate difference, but City were holding out and the minutes were ticking by. Then Gow, who had twice been caught in possession, chased back and unwisely fouled Ardiles about four yards outside the box. The ensuing free-kick was rolled to Hoddle, who clipped it over the wall. Corrigan seemed to have it covered. But Hutchison, quick to spot the danger, had peeled off the wall and suddenly found the ball deflected off his shoulder into the opposite side of the goal.

The pace slowed considerably in extra time, and players were going down like guardsmen in a heatwave. There was no further score, however, and so the game went to a replay, also at Wembley, with the unpopular FA decision that, in the event of another draw, there would be a penalty decider.

The replay turned out to be a thriller, and fortunately

Left: After 90 minutes and with the score tied at 1-1, the players receive treatment for cramp.

Right: Ricky Villa (centre) lashes a loose ball into the net to put Spurs one up after only seven minutes of the replay.

there was no need to resort to penalties. Despite injury scares, the teams fielded the same sides, with the exception of City substitute Dennis Tueart. Burkinshaw showed great courage in keeping faith with Villa.

After seven minutes, Ardiles produced a delightful piece of brilliance on the left before shooting against team-mate Archibald's legs. The blond striker managed to control the ball and get in a shot, which was gallantly blocked by Corrigan, only to hit Caton and fall just right for Villa, who gratefully swept it into the net.

Three minutes later, City scored a spectacular equaliser. Hutchison headed square to Mackenzie 22 yards out, and the young giant hit an unstoppable volley past Aleksic.

Spurs continued to press, and their midfield was moving sweetly. Hoddle's probing passes were giving the City defenders all kinds of trouble, and Crooks and Archibald were dragging them out wide for Villa to come through the middle. Yet it was City who took the lead, after five minutes of the second half. Bennett was brought down in the box, and Reeves converted the penalty.

Tempers began to flare, but Ardiles and Hoddle stayed cool and continued to play football. And it was a typical piece of Hoddle flair that made the Spurs equaliser after 70 minutes. He flicked the ball up over the advancing City defence, and as Archibald, just onside, controlled the ball, his striking partner Crooks pounced and fired it home.

Then, seven minutes later, Tony Galvin on the left touchline squared the ball to Villa. Full of confidence now, the exciting Argentinian ran at the City defence. Forced outside by Caton, he took the ball past both Caton and Ransom, before cutting it back past Caton again and holding it for an agonising second before hammering it past Corrigan.

It was a fitting goal with which to win what had become a classic hundredth Cup final.

Villa, the matchwinner, and Hoddle (left), the inspiration, celebrate with the Cup.

The PFA Awards

Above: The Ipswich 1-2-3: John Wark (left), Frans Thijssen (right, with captain Mick Mills), and Paul Mariner (centre).
Below: Tony Currie (QPR), one of only three players to break West Ham's monopoly of the 'Second Division select XI'.

Ipswich players dominated the Player of the Year award at the annual Professional Footballers' Association dinner, coming first, second, and third in the voting. It was a tale of a Scot, a Dutchman, and an Englishman!

Player of the Year was John Wark, their Scottish midfielder with the gift for goals, especially in European competition. Not far behind him in the ballot of the Football League players was Frans Thijssen, who with fellow Dutch star Arnold Muhren provided the Suffolk club's midfield craft. Third was England striker Paul Mariner, enjoying one of his best ever seasons.

'Young Player of the Year' was Gary Shaw, Aston Villa's exciting striker, with Sammy Lee of Liverpool and Steve Moran of Southampton the runners-up. Middlesbrough provided two players in the first six – Craig Johnston and David Hodgson.

The Merit Award for special services to football went to John Trollope, who set a new record of League appearances for one club during the season (Swindon Town). Previous winners include such illustrious names as Bobby Charlton, Sir Matt Busby, Tom Finney, and Bill Shankly.

It is customary for each division to nominate a best team from all its players, and the most noteworthy selection was that of Division II. It contained eight West Ham players! The team was (West Ham unless otherwise indicated): Phil Parkes; Ray Stewart, Billy Bonds, Alvin Martin, Ray O'Brien (Notts County); Tony Currie (QPR), Trevor Brooking, Alan Devonshire; Paul Goddard, David Cross, and Terry Curran (Sheffield Wed.).

John Wark Ipswich

Gary Shaw Aston Villa

Gary Shaw rides a tackle from Ipswich's Russell Osman.

Villa's Front Men

Young Player of the Year Gary Shaw and 'old timer' Peter Withe team up to make one of the most exciting striking forces in the country

Aston Villa's emergence once again as a force in English football was due in no small part to the fine understanding built up by their new striking partnership of Gary Shaw and Peter Withe. With Tony Morley feeding them with crosses from the wing and Dennis Mortimer and Gordon Cowans prompting from midfield, the striking force enjoyed a wonderful service.

Gary Shaw, voted 'Young Player of the Year' by his fellow professionals, had been Villa's leading scorer in 1979–80, his first full season, with 9 goals in 28 League games, but had dried up towards the end of the season. The much-travelled Peter Withe had been signed from Newcastle United in the close season for a club record fee of £500,000. Born in Liverpool, he had previously played as an amateur for several clubs before coming late to League football with Wolves and then Birmingham and Nottingham Forest.

The modest Shaw attributes much of his own scoring success to his older partner, and felt that he should have scored more goals from the countless knock-downs and lay-backs he received. More than that, he also acknowledged the protection Withe gave him from robust defenders with his height and strength.

Nevertheless, no one could accuse Shaw of holding back. He consistently showed great courage in going for goal, and tremendous confidence, too. His inventiveness and willingness to try something different made him a huge favourite with the fans, and his Under-21 and 'B' team honours must surely be followed by full internationals.

The season has been a personal triumph, too, for the tall Withe, nearing 30. He had played a considerable part in Forest's League and European Cup triumphs of the late 70s, but two seasons in the Second Division with Newcastle had looked like providing an anti-climax to his career. Then Ron Saunders came in with his bid, and Withe justified the confidence his new manager had shown in him. He was rewarded with a League Championship medal and his first England cap.

This is good news for Villa, as their England international Brian Little sadly had to retire from the game because of injury. But with Shaw and Withe up front now, they have one of the most exciting striking forces in the country.

Peter Withe screens the ball from Paul Hart of Leeds.

An early clash between the two clubs who would fight out the First Division Championship, Ipswich and Aston Villa. In the centre are Terry Butcher of Ipswich and Dennis Mortimer and Allan Evans of Villa. Ipswich won this one with a goal by Frans Thijssen. They also won the return near the end of the season, but Villa won the title.

Record Breakers

While Liverpool were breaking all kinds of records in the late 1970s and early 1980s, their manager Bob Paisley was himself creating a little personal football history. For in 1980, he won the Manager of the Year award for a record fourth time.

Bell's Scotch Whisky inaugurated the award in 1966, when it went, appropriately enough, to Jock Stein, manager of Scottish champions Celtic. Paisley broke the record of Leeds United's Don Revie, a three-time winner.

John Trollope (right) receiving a loyalty award from Jimmy Dickinson.

On 18 October 1980, John Trollope chalked up his 765th League appearance for Swindon Town, thus beating the record for one club, set 15 years earlier by Jimmy Dickinson of Portsmouth.

Full-back Trollope, who had made his debut for Swindon in August 1960, had relinquished his first-team place two seasons before in order to take charge of the youth team, and had not played for over a season when he was asked to help out. He kept his place long enough to beat the record, and took his League tally to 770 matches before he finally retired at 37.

On 9 September 1980, Eamonn Collins became the youngest player to turn out for a Football League club in a first-class match. He was 14 years and 323 days when player-manager Alan Ball took him off the Blackpool substitute's bench and put him on for the last 15 minutes of the Anglo-Scot Cup tie against Kilmarnock.

Born in Dublin, he was able to sign for Blackpool because of the Irish law that allows children to leave school before 16 if they have a job to go

to. Blackpool, however, had to arrange private tuition for him as required by British law.

An extremely modest lad, Eamonn enjoyed the experience (Blackpool won 2-1) but has kept his feet firmly on the ground. It may be a little longer before the young striker hits the headlines again, but the little bit of football history he made that Tuesday night in September will keep his name in the record books for a long time to come.

Liverpool's remarkable home record was finally broken after three years by, of all teams, relegation-haunted Leicester City. For 85 matches Liverpool had remained unbeaten at Anfield. Their record run included 63 League matches and various cup-ties in domestic and European competition, and covered a period of 3 years and 10 days.

Then along came Leicester on 31 January 1981, languishing at the very bottom of the table. They gave Liverpool a half-time lead with an 'own goal', but in the second half scored twice.

The end of a record run: Leicester players celebrate while Liverpool's Ray Kennedy stands dumbstruck.

Sammy Lee
Liverpool

Kenny Sansom Arsenal

A £1,000,000 Success

Sansom gives good value

Of all the million-pound transfer men, Kenny Sansom is perhaps the only one who has been an immediate and unqualified success with his new club. Moving to Arsenal from Crystal Palace at the beginning of the season in a controversial deal that involved an exchange with Clive Allen, who had not yet had a chance to show his own worth, Sansom straight away slotted in to the Highbury defence.

Unlike most of the other million-pound men, Sansom, as a left-back, did not have to prove himself with goals. But it is in attack that he is seen at his best. At Highbury, he quickly struck up a fine relationship with their wide-playing midfielder Graham Rix. Their combination in bringing the ball out of defence has been a feature of the Arsenal game, and Sansom himself is always eager to get into forward positions. Apart from putting over excellent crosses, he often makes dangerous forays into the opposing penalty box, with the ball or in support.

A goal he will want to forget, however, is the one he put in the Arsenal net in the Cup against Everton, which effectively put paid to Arsenal's hopes of reaching Wembley for a fourth successive season. But even

Kenny in World Cup action for England against Switzerland.

this could not diminish the esteem in which he is held by the Highbury fans. This, of course, is because Kenny is such an exciting player, ever adventurous and always ready to improvise. His quick thinking and tim-

ing are just as evident in defence as in attack, and his reading of the game makes up for his lack of height.

No one at Highbury doubts that Arsenal made a good buy in Sansom, and his displays for England suggest that he will hold his international place for many years to come.

Behind Closed Doors

West Ham fans pay the penalty for the mindless minority

Above: No crowd trouble for this 'Bobby' to deal with as West Ham take on Castilla in front of empty terraces, a result of their fans misbehaviour in Spain.

Right: There's no great roar to greet David Cross's hat-trick, but he celebrates just the same.

The strangest match that took place all season must be West Ham's home leg in the European Cup-Winners Cup against Castilla of Spain. Because of the shameful behaviour of some of the West Ham fans in the first leg in Madrid, UEFA fined the club and decreed that the return should be held behind closed doors.

As a result, an eerie atmosphere pervaded Upton Park on Wednesday night, October 1st, when the two Second Division clubs met, the Spaniards with a 3-1 lead from their home tie.

West Ham had done everything in their power to prevent trouble in Madrid. Tickets were made available only to registered supporters, who were photographed and their passport numbers noted. And West Ham captain Billy Bonds wrote to each ticket-holder stressing the need for sensible behaviour. But there was nothing the club could do about the so-called fans who travelled independently, bought their tickets in Madrid, and then, no doubt unable to hold their duty-free liquor, disgraced not only themselves but their club and their country.

In addition to the fine, West Ham lost the revenue from their home tie. But football won in the end, for West Ham treated the 300 or so officials to a fine display, and took an overall lead with three goals before half-time. A second-half goal from Castilla forced extra time, though, but two goals from David Cross gave him his hat-trick, and West Ham went through to the second round 6-4 on aggregate.

Right: Two Irish defenders whose absence for spells during the season was felt at Arsenal — Pat Jennings of Northern Ireland and David O'Leary of the Republic.

Below: Scotland began their World Cup campaign at Hampden Park with a game against Portugal. Gordon Strachan slams a free-kick against the Portuguese wall in their goalless draw.

Terry Connor
Leeds Utd.

David Hodgson
Middlesbrough

Justin Fashanu
Norwich

Soccer 'Olympics'

Below: Gymnastics from John Hollins, the rings, perhaps, or even the high bar.

Above: There's no doubt that Sammy McIlroy (right) is heading for goal, watched by Manchester United team-mate Steve Coppell. But when footballers 'take to the air' they often look as if they are participating in other sports.

Below: Arsenal's Steve Gatting (left) and Coventry's Garry Thompson show all the coordination and balance of ice dancers as they land in perfect symmetry.

Above: Gary Birtles appears to be hurdling over Joe Jordan's knees.
Below: It's Garry Thompson again, doing the long jump with help from Arsenal's Willie Young.

Above: West Ham's Alvin Martin uses a different technique to hurdle Liverpool's Ray Kennedy.
Below: Not much doubt about what Garth Crooks of Spurs is doing — the pole vault.

Steve Archibald Spurs

Top Scorer

Slotting in at Spurs

Steve Archibald's first season in English football was an unqualified success. A star of Aberdeen's title-winning side of 1979-80, he went to Spurs for £800,000 but with several question marks as to his ability to fit into the more competitive game south of the border.

He immediately slotted in with Spurs' other new signing Garth Crooks up front to form a lethal striking partnership. But it was the former Stoke man who took the initial honours. Gradually, though, Archibald built up a reputation for finishing that was second to none in the First Division. As he steadily knocked in the goals and rose to the top of the scoring charts, the rest of his game flourished.

Steve Archibald is not

Above: New Spurs signing Steve Archibald gave notice of his intentions with a fine performance against Forest early in the season. He gave both Kenny Burns (left) and Peter Shilton (right) a hard time.
Below: Archibald and striking partner Garth Crooks are just as in step on the field as they are in training.

merely a goalscoring machine, he is a fine footballer, too. And he chooses to play his best football in the box, where it really matters. Cool and sharp, he is always alive to the half-chance, and never afraid to take an opponent on. Very rarely off target, he makes opposing keepers work for their money, and they have great difficulty in anticipating his shots.

Apart from his understanding with Crooks, he has benefited enormously from the defence-splitting services of midfielders Ardiles and Hoddle. His fine form for Spurs has helped his international career, and neither Andy Gray nor Kenny Dalglish can feel sure of their place in Scotland's front line with Steve Archibald around.

The Road to Spain

British hopes enjoy mixed fortunes in the World Cup qualifying matches

In the quest for a place in the 1982 World Cup to be staged in Spain in June and July, all four home countries as well as the Republic of Ireland kept their chances alive in the first rounds of qualifying matches.

Of the five, Wales could be most satisfied with their progress. They opened up with four straight wins in Group 3, the 1-0 defeat of Czechoslovakia in Cardiff with a David Giles goal being a vital victory. Picking up full points from Iceland and particularly Turkey did their chances no harm at all. Their 4-0 victory in Reykjavic in the opening match in the group was Iceland's biggest home defeat for seven years.

With Wrexham's Dai Davies in goal (he broke Jack Kelsey's record number of caps for a Welsh goalkeeper during the season), Brian Flynn creating in midfield, and Leighton James back to his dazzling best on the wing, Wales were building into their best side since the days of John and Mel Charles in the 1950s. Mel's son Jeremy, built in the mould of his father and uncle, made his international debut in the match against Czechoslovakia.

The unluckiest of the five countries must surely by the Republic of Ireland. Drawn in the most difficult of the European groups, along

A headed goal from Paul Mariner (right) helped England to a 2-1 win over the Swiss at Wembley ... but manager Ron Greenwood realised the job of qualifying for Spain would not be an easy one.

with Belgium, France, and Holland, they beat the Dutch 2-1 and held European runners-up Belgium to a 1-1 draw, both in Dublin. They led the table going into the return match in Brussels, and just before half-time appeared to take the lead when Frank Stapleton converted a quick free-kick from his former Arsenal colleague Liam Brady. But the referee inexplicably disal-

lowed the score, and Jan Ceulemans snatched the winner in the dying minutes to put Belgium on top of Group 2. With France and Holland breathing down their necks having games in hand, the Irish have their work cut out to qualify, but are still in there with a chance.

Scotland and Northern Ireland were drawn together in Group 6, with Portugal the only other serious contenders. It soon became evident that at least one of the home countries would qualify. And when Northern Ireland beat Portugal 1-0 in Belfast with a header from Watford's Gerry Armstrong,

If Liverpool stars Kenny Dalglish (left) and Graeme Souness (right), in action against Portugal, could consistently reproduce their club form for Scotland, manager Jock Stein's cares would be halved.

it increased the chances of both getting to Spain. Boosted by their Home Championship triumph in 1980, the Irish feared nobody, and their 3-0 defeat of Sweden was a classy performance, crowned with a spectacular 35-yard goal from Manchester United full-back Jimmy Nicholl. His namesake, Southampton's Chris Nicholl, has been an inspiration at the centre of the defence and Middlesbrough's Jim Platt ably deputised for the evergreen Pat Jennings in goal when called upon.

Before they beat Portugal, the Irish had given the Scots a fright at Hampden, taking a 1-0 lead in 70 minutes through Burnley's Billy Hamilton, but John Wark equalised for the Scots five minutes later and the loss of a home point did not dent Scottish hopes unduly. They had chalked up 1-0 victories in Sweden and Israel, and despite being held to a goalless draw by Portugal at Hampden were sitting pretty at the top of the group. Injuries, however, had made it difficult for Jock Stein to produce a settled team. And even though they could call on strikers of the calibre of Kenny Dalglish, Steve Archibald, Andy Gray, and Joe Jordan, their initial problem was scoring goals.

England's early performances in Group 4 left a great deal to be desired. Injuries

and loss of form by key players made it difficult for Ron Greenwood to fashion a settled side. No one got carried away by their opening 4-0 victory over Norway at Wembley, and their 2-1 defeat in Romania soon afterwards was a blow. A Tony Woodcock equaliser in the second half appeared to have ensured a point for England, but they went down to a highly doubtful penalty near the end.

Experiencing his worst ever season for injuries, England's captain Kevin Keegan missed the first half of their World Cup programme. But this was far

Former Spurs and Welsh centre-half Mike England quietly built up a promising Welsh side that gave the USSR and Czechoslovakia plenty to think about in Group 3.

from Greenwood's only problem. Lack of penetration up front must be his biggest concern. Despite a remarkable recovery from injury, Trevor Francis has been unable to recapture his sharpest form, and Paul Mariner has not been able to reproduce his Ipswich form for England. In midfield, too, Terry McDermott is not nearly so effective for his country as he is for Liverpool, and a long lay-off through injury did not help Ray Wilkins. Greenwood has taken the opportunity of blooding Tottenham's Glenn Hoddle and Arsenal's Graham Rix in midfield, where their inventiveness holds out great promise for the future, and West Bromwich's Bryan Robson has been a revelation both in midfield and as a semi-sweeper. In attack, England's hopes might rest on the return of wingers to the international scene. Peter Barnes's performance in a friendly against Brazil was enormously encouraging, and Steve Coppell is always dangerous when given more scope to attack.

England's inability to beat a defence-minded Romanian side at Wembley was depressing, and their defeat in Switzerland almost catastrophic. But they put themselves right back in the reckoning with a confidence-boosting 3-1 win in Budapest over Hungary.

World Cup Quiz

As the qualifiers for the 1982 World Cup emerge from the preliminary groups, everyone's attention in football will be focused on the finals to be held in Spain.

Most previous finals have had 16 competing countries. For the first World Cup, held in Uruguay in 1930, there were only·13. The 1982 finals will be the biggest yet, with more teams competing over a longer period than ever before. Twenty-two qualifiers will join the hosts, Spain, and the holders, Argentina, in a competition that will take a month and 52 matches to complete.

Some people think this is too much football and that there will be too many of the weaker nations in the finals. On the other hand, the World Cup takes place only every four years, and it is good for the lesser footballing continents to have a wider interest in the finals. And the so-called weaker sides have produced plenty of surprises in the past.

Test your knowledge of the World Cup by answering the questions posed underneath the pictures. You will find the answers on page 57.

1   **1930**

2   **1958**

3   **1966**

(1) A goal from the first World Cup final. Who were the teams and what was the result?

(2) Another World Cup final. Who is the player in the dark shirt and what was the result?

(3) What team is this and why the joy and celebrations? Who eventually eliminated them?

36

4   **1966**

(4) This is a famous incident from the 1966 final. What led up to it and what was the referee's decision?

(5) Another final, another celebration. Who scored this goal and what was the final result?

(6) This is from a qualifying match. Who is heading the ball and what is significant about the incident?

(7) Here is an incident from the last World Cup final. Who is heading the ball and with what result?

5   **1970**

6   **1973**

7   **1978**

Managerial Merry-go-round

Brown | Allison | Walley | Docherty | Venables | Gradi

Half-way through the season, the chairmen of the 92 Football League clubs announced a 'gentleman's agreement' to the effect that 'no club will take another club's manager during the course of a season'. This was none too soon, because the speed with which managerial doors had been opening and closing was becoming reminiscent of a French bedroom farce.

With Tommy Docherty out of the country, having been sacked by Queen's Park Rangers, it was the turn of Malcolm Allison to take the stage.

His success with Manchester City in the 1960s was a result of his partnership with Joe Mercer, and when he took over sole charge City began to decline. Despite this, he was appointed manager again in 1979, ran through millions of pounds in the transfer market... and took City to the bottom of the First Division!

Many thought that City chairman Peter Swales should have resigned, be-

cause he was responsible for appointing Allison, but he decided that it was Allison who should go. Thus the managerial merry-go-round began...

Manchester City chairman Peter Swales (left) welcomes new manager John Bond, who came hot-foot from Norwich, where Ken Brown took over. This left Malcolm Allison out in the cold, but not for long, because Tommy Docherty had been sacked by QPR, and Terry Venables left Palace to take over at QPR, leaving Ernie Walley in charge of Palace, until they brought in Allison, even though

he had been manager before, from 1973 to 1976, when he took them from Division I to Division III. But before Allison had a chance to repeat this feat, Wimbledon chairman Ron Noades took over Palace and replaced him with Wimbledon manager Dario Gradi...

Confused? Well, you may be forgiven for thinking this is a synopsis of a typical episode of TV's 'Soap'.

Light Relief at the Palace

Flanagan and Allen top the bill for a brief season

Crystal Palace had a season they will want to forget. But there was one brief period at the start when hope abounded. Million-pound Queen's Park Rangers goal-scorer Clive Allen had signed for them via Arsenal and joined another scoring star, Mike Flanagan, up front. Flanagan and Allen were back at the Palace.

After a shaky start, Palace came good in their third match, beating Middles-brough 5-2, and Clive Allen scored a hat-trick. Flanagan scored in the next game, a 3-0 away win over Bolton in the League Cup. But there was very little to cheer after that, as things gradually turned sour at the Palace. Manager Terry Venables left for Queen's Park Rangers and Mike Flanagan soon fol-lowed him there. More managerial changes and the loss of his place soured things even more for Allen (at the end of the season he was transferred back to QPR). Palace were doomed to relegation.

No, not a happy season for Palace fans — but when they look back on it, they can still smile at the time when Flanagan and Allen were the star turn at the Palace.

Mike Flanagan (right) congrat-ulates Clive Allen on his first goal for Palace. It was the first of a hat-trick he scored against Middlesbrough.

Mike and Clive go along with the joke and dress up as their old music-hall namesakes, Bud Flanagan and Chesney Allen (inset), who used to star at the Victoria Palace as part of the Crazy Gang. Anyone who walked into Selhurst Park dur-ing their managerial shake-ups could have been excused for thinking the Crazy Gang were at work!

Soccer Duels

The clashes that win matches

Although football is a team game, dozens of times during a match it develops into a confrontation between one player from each side – a soccer duel. The winners of most of these 'mini-matches', or 'one-against-one situations' to use the technical jargon, will often be the match-winners.

Below: Forest's Stuart Gray (left) and Manchester United's Joe Jordan seem to be tying themselves in knots while the ball runs free.

Below left: Mick Lyons of Everton appears more concerned with stopping Southampton's Charlie George than with the ball, and both players have their eyes shut.

Bottom left: There are of course, unfair confrontations, as Eric Gates of Ipswich finds out when he is brought down by Steve Lovell of Palace.

Above: Liverpool's Ray Kennedy skilfully screens the ball from Dennis Mortimer of Aston Villa while he gets in a cross.

Below: A fine tackle by Paul Miller of Spurs looks like preventing Arsenal's Alan Sunderland from getting in his cross.

Above: It's anyone's ball as Ian Bailey of Middlesbrough (left) and Manchester City's Kevin Reeves strive for possession.

Below: Garth Crooks of Spurs (left) is dispossessed by young Reuben Agboola, who made his debut for Southampton during the season.

Euro~Quiz

British clubs have a fine record of success in all the European competitions. The pictures on these pages are all British goals in successful finals or celebrations after a triumph. Can you answer the questions? The answers are on page 57.

(1) This is the 1965 European Cup-Winners Cup final. Who is scoring (he's on the right), what was the result, and where did it take place?

(2) Where is this celebration, who is the team, and what have they won? There's a clue in the trophy itself, one of the biggest in football.

(3) This happy scene took place a year after the previous one. Who are the players and why are they so jubilant?

(4) Who is heading this goal? What is the competition and what was the result?

(5) Who scored this penalty? What is the competition and what was the result?

(6) What is happening here? Who are the teams involved and what was the result?

(7) Who is scoring this goal? What was the competition and what was the result?

It's a Goal!

Goalscoring affects players in different ways. Usually at least one arm goes up to salute the effort, but there the similarity ends. Maybe it is possible to determine a player's character from his goalscoring celebrations, as can be done with handwriting. See what you make of this lot!

Above: England's Terry McDermott (left) and Eric Gates see the funny side of goalscor-ing, even in a World Cup qualifying match. **Below: Terry Hibbitt scores for Newcastle** and demonstrates restrained glee, with fists and teeth clenched.

Nikki Jovanovic (above) of Manchester United exhibits childlike joy, while Southampton's Mick Channon (below) may not have taken out a copyright on his windmilling action, but it's his trademark nevertheless, and the fans love it.

Above: Paul Mariner (centre) of Ipswich milks the applause with a certain modesty . . .

. . . while goalscoring for teammate John Wark (below) is a serious business.

What's in a Name?

Which Walsh is which?

(1) A Welsh Walsh!

(2) An Irishman in Portugal.

(3) And an Englishman — versatile performer for the Wanderers.

More than one Walsh hit the headlines during the season. With the help of the clues provided, fit the first names to the footballing Walshes (no relations) who made the news or perhaps just kept plugging away. The answers are on page 57.

(4) A wet Walsh, but not on the field. Athletic, too.

(5) A promising newcomer to the First Division.

The League Cup

**Dramatic draw at Wembley followed by classic replay at Villa Park —
Then Liverpool win**

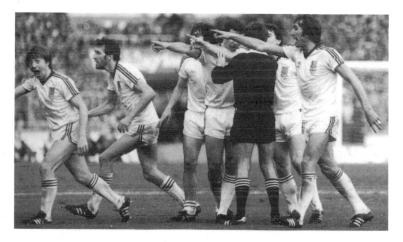

At last, Liverpool won the only domestic competition that had eluded them — the League Cup. Second Division champions West Ham, themselves no strangers to Wembley, fought well and courageously and took the 'Reds' to a replay. But in the end Liverpool put on one of the finest displays of the season at Villa Park and deservedly won the trophy.

Yet in a season in which they often fell short of the high standards they had set in previous years, they began their League Cup campaign with a Second Round first-leg defeat at Fourth Division Bradford City. It was a different story at Anfield, though, and with three home draws to follow Liverpool found themselves in the semi-finals without extending themselves.

West Ham, on the other hand, after brushing Burnley aside 6-0 on aggregate in the Second Round, had a tougher ride, with three one-goal victories, culminating in their defeat of Spurs at Upton Park with a late David Cross goal.

The semi-finals really brought the League Cup to life. Coventry, having reached their first ever semi-final in any major competition, entertained West Ham at Highfield Road in the first leg — and proceeded to treat them to a two-goal start! A goalkeeping error and a Garry Thompson own goal before half-time appeared to have put paid to Coventry's chances. But a marvellous second-half revival in which Thompson scored two for his own side gave them a one-goal lead to take to Upton Park. There, in another thrilling tie, Paul Goddard hit a beautiful equaliser after an hour and

Jimmy Neighbour scored the winner two minutes from time.

Meanwhile, Liverpool were not having things their own way against a revived Manchester City side that had been playing some of the finest football in the First Division under their new manager John Bond after early relegation worries. City, desperately unlucky to finish one down after their home leg, put up a fine performance at Anfield, but a 1-1 draw was not enough.

The final at Wembley was a great disappointment, saved only by its dramatic finale. Liverpool had the best of the first half, and were unlucky when Sammy Lee shot in off a post only to have the goal disallowed because Colin Irwin was offside. Phil Parkes made a brilliant one-handed stop from a point-blank Kenny Dalglish header, despite going the wrong way.

In the second half West Ham came more into the game and Goddard wasted their best chance when he was wild with an attempted lob over the advancing Clemence. In the first period of extra time, Jimmy Case,

Ray Stewart sends Clemence the wrong way (left) and leaps in elation and relief (right) after **scoring West Ham's dramatic equaliser from the spot with the last kick of the match.**

who had come on for Steve Heighway after 65 minutes, had a purple patch in which he slammed a twenty-yarder against the bar and went close another couple of times. In the second period of extra time, West Ham brought on their substitute Stuart Pearson for Goddard, but the game was progressing predictably to a replay when suddenly all the drama was condensed into the last three minutes.

First, Liverpool scored probably the most controversial goal of the season.

Alan Kennedy hammered a poor clearance past Parkes from the edge of the box, but Lee was lying in an offside position near the penalty spot. Referee Clive Thomas gave a goal, judging that the motionless Lee was not seeking to gain an advantage. But there is little doubt that Lee was interfering with play, albeit unintentionally, and thus should have been given offside. The West Ham players surrounded the referee to protest, and Thomas later regretted not going straight

to his linesman, in order to let the West Ham players know that he had seen him flagging. But that was not the point. It was the referee's decision, and Thomas was in the best position to decide whether Lee was interfering with play. In the event, he almost certainly made the wrong decision, but even the best referees make mistakes in the heat of the moment. This mistake should in no way be allowed to diminish the reputation of one of the finest referees in the world.

Fortunately, justice was done. Only a couple of minutes after the furore had died down, West Ham 'came back from the dead'. Alan Devonshire was hacked down a foot outside the box, and Clemence made a magnificent save from the resultant free kick, turning Ray Stewart's goal-bound shot round the post for a corner. With only seconds remaining, Neighbour placed the corner on Alvin Martin's head, and West Ham were again denied the equaliser by a fingertip. This time, however, it was not the keeper's but Terry Mc-Dermott's — an indisputable penalty. With the last kick of the match, Stewart

One of the finest goals of the season — Kenny Dalglish about to hook home Liverpool's equaliser in the replayed final, with Billy Bonds (left) and Geoff Pike looking on helplessly.

dramatically tucked a low shot inside the right-hand post to earn West Ham a replay.

The replay took place 18 days later on the evening of April 1st. Alvin Martin passed a late fitness test for West Ham, who were unchanged, but for Liverpool, Case and Ian Rush replaced the injured Souness and Heighway and Phil Thompson came back after injury to captain the side and replace Irwin. Without him, Liverpool's defence had appeared shaky, and his presence made a great difference to their confidence.

Liverpool dominated the game from the start, yet they went a goal down in nine minutes to what was virtually West Ham's first attack. Jimmy Neighbour raced down the right wing, skipped past a lunging Hansen tackle, made for the bye-line and from just outside the box placed a perfect cross on to Goddard's head at the near post. Clemence could only help the powerful deflection into the net.

Many teams would have crumbled at such an early reverse. But Liverpool continued to play football, if a little frantic at times, and they maintained control of midfield with Sammy Lee outstanding. Up front, Kenny Dalglish was always dangerous, twisting and turning and bringing the best out of Phil Parkes in West Ham's goal. Next to him, Rush, a Welsh international, but pulled out of the reserves to play only his second game in the first team, gave a polished performance, and was unlucky to see a fine attempt hit the woodwork.

It was a superb Dalglish goal that put Liverpool on level terms. Rush laid the ball back to Terry McDermott outside the box, and he chipped it back to the corner of the goal area as Dalglish ran through under pressure to hook the ball brilliantly before it touched the ground past a helpless Parkes. Three minutes later, he was in the action again, forcing a corner on the right. From Case's kick, Hansen rose above the West Ham defence to power a header towards the left-hand corner. Billy Bonds tried to intercept it, but only succeeded in deflecting it with his thigh past Parkes and another defender on the line. It was the winning goal.

West Ham improved in the second half, with Brooking and Devonshire coming into the game. Brooking made and just missed a good chance near the end, and Cross was also just wide of the far post with a last-minute attempt to take the game

into extra time and a possible penalty decider. But it was a brave effort on their part even to stay in the game with Liverpool playing such fine football. The match was a splendid advertisement for soccer, and Liverpool's victory ensured their 18th successive season in Europe. The only argument was who scored the winning goal — Bonds or Hansen?

Wembley, 14 March, att. 100,000
Liverpool (0)(0) 1 West Ham (0)(0) 1
A. Kennedy   Stewart (pen)
Liverpool (4-4-2): Clemence; Neal, Irwin, Hansen, A. Kennedy; Lee, McDermott, Souness, R. Kennedy; Dalglish, Heighway (sub. Case 65 min.)
West Ham (4-3-3): Parkes; Stewart, Bonds, Martin, Lampard; Brooking, Devonshire, Pike; Neighbour, Goddard (sub. Pearson 109 min.), Cross.

Villa Park, 1 April, att. 36,693
Liverpool (2) 2 West Ham (1) 1
Dalglish, Hansen Goddard
Liverpool (4-4-2): Clemence; Neal, Thompson, Hansen, A. Kennedy; Case, McDermott, Lee, R. Kennedy; Dalglish, Rush. (Sub. Irwin not used)
West Ham (4-3-3): As for Wembley game (Pearson sub. 83 min.)

The unfortunate Bonds (left) sticks out a leg to stop an Alan Hansen header, and succeeds only in deflecting the ball past his keeper for Liverpool's winning goal.

49

So Far, So Good...

Liam Brady in Italy

When Liam Brady left Arsenal to try his luck in Italy, there were many who doubted his wisdom. He was just reaching the top as a star of a successful club and was captain of the Republic of Ireland. Despite his undisputed talents there were doubts about his ability to settle down in Italian football. His performances for Juventus, however, have won him nothing but praise and admiration, and he has become one of the leading lights of Italian football.

Because of regulations governing transfers within the Common Market, Juventus signed Brady for a 'give-away' fee of about £400,000. At prevailing British prices, he was worth, three, four, or even five times that. So Arsenal 'lost' a million pounds on the deal. They lost more than that, though, because they were deprived of the man who held them together, the midfield gen-

Above left: Brady is welcomed by his new team-mates at Juventus. Above right: Married in the summer, Liam and his bride Sarah quickly settled into Italian life. Below: On the field, too, Brady settled into the Italian style and soon became a favourite.

eral who made the others tick and who could turn a game with one jinking run or with a deadly 'bent' chip to a team-mate.

Brady was an immediate hit with Juventus, settling down well with the players and endearing himself to the fans. It was the ease with which he adapted himself, both to the Italian way of life and to their style of football

that surprised most people. For these have been the stumbling blocks of many Italian football immigrants of the past. Brady, however, knew what to expect. So he determined to make every effort, both on and off the field, to fit in with the Italian ways.

In six months he had mastered the language sufficiently to give interviews or talk on the telephone. His calming influence on the field and his vision in midfield lifted Juventus, who had been going through a bad period. And Brady was soon enjoying both his football and his life in Italy.

The initial report on Brady's progress, then, must be, to borrow from his autobiography: 'So far, so good . . .' There is still a way to go before Liam Brady can be classed as one of the 'all-time greats', but he has done his chances no harm by his adventure in Italy.

Transfer Quiz

(1) Paul Mariner of Ipswich tracks a Crystal Palace player. Who is the player on the ball and to which team was he transferred?

(2) The Forest player (left) being challenged by John Hollins was transferred in February for £250,000. To which club?

(3) Who is this player and what was unusual about his transfer?

(4) Who is tackling Ricardo Villa of Spurs and which club did he go to?

(5) Who's putting sugar in Clive Allen's tea at training and where did he come from? What position does he play?

(6) Arsenal's Alan Sunderland seems to be saying 'make me an offer'. Who is on the left and between which two clubs was he transferred?

Answers on page 57

Looking for Wingers

Above: Vince Hilaire, exciting and incisive, has suffered from the upheavals at Crystal Palace, but he could realise his enormous potential when he settles down again.

Below: Steve Coppell, an England international, is used mostly as a wide midfielder. In this role, he is always in the action, but some think his talents are wasted and that he should be played as a true winger. There are certainly few players who are better at making for the bye-line or cutting in for a shot.

The best Christmas present England manager Ron Greenwood could receive would be a world-class winger. British club football just does not seem to produce them any more. When England won the World Cup in 1966, they were called the 'Wingless Wonders'. It was not a strategy dreamed up by the then manager, Alf Ramsey, but a formation he finished up with because he could not find wingers of sufficient class. This problem still continued.

Many teams play with just twin strikers up front. And the obsession with getting men 'behind the ball' means that wing men usually spend most of their time wide in midfield anyway. As a result, there is less opportunity to use their wing skills. The wings now are used more by overlapping full-backs.

Nevertheless, there are signs that wingers might be coming back into fashion in British football. Whereas, a few seasons ago, you could

Above: John Robertson (left), a Scottish international and stalwart of Nottingham Forest's domestic and European successes, relies more on timing and acceleration to get past his man than on basic speed. He is difficult to shake off the ball, and his crossing and shooting are deadly accurate.

Below: Peter Barnes would be a world-beater if he added consistency to his speed, body swerve, and acceleration. The most capped of England's current wingers, he has yet to establish a permanent international place.

count barely half a dozen true wing men in the First Division for instance, now there are young wingers popping up all over the place. Whether they develop into world-class players is another matter, but for the sake of our international success — and, of course, for football in general — we can only hope they do.

Let us take a look at some of these young hopefuls, and at one or two of the more established wing men who have kept the flag flying, so to speak, in the last few seasons.

Below: Aston Villa's left-winger Tony Morley has many admirers who would like to see him in an England shirt. He carries the ball well and has scored some spectacular goals on the run with his lethal right foot.

Above: Tall and heavily built, Scottish international Alan Brazil (right) plays a front-running role for Ipswich and is particularly effective out wide, but cannot be classed as an out-and-out winger.

Below: Another Ipswich man, Kevin O'Callaghan has had few chances to show his paces since signing from Millwall for £250,000. But his performances, chiefly as substitute, have been full of promise.

Above: Leighton James's wing skills were a prominent feature in the success of both Wales and Swansea.

Steve Moran

Southampton's shooting star

When Lawrie McMenemy first arrived at Southampton, he used to watch his 11-year-old son playing Sunday soccer. On a particularly wet day, one lad was slithering about and falling over more than most, and at half-time the Southampton manager found out why – he did not have proper football boots, but was wearing trainers entirely unsuited to the muddy conditions. McMenemy told the boy: 'You get a hat-trick in the second half, and I'll buy you a pair of boots.'

Before the others had finished their half-time refreshments, the boy had placed the ball on the centre-spot, raring to go. 'He then proceeded to score the quickest hat-trick I've ever seen,' said McMenemy. 'After each goal, he looked up at me and gave a thumbs-up sign, and on the Monday morning he was outside the sports shop before it opened!'

The young lad's name was Steve Moran, and seven years later he began to repay McMenemy's kindness. Coming into the Southampton side in the 1980–81 season because of injuries to others, he scored 16 goals in

Only 1·71m tall but a glutton for goals, 20-year-old Southampton front-runner Steve Moran enjoyed a highly successful first season.

his first 19 appearances (including two as substitute). He retained his place because of his goalscoring exploits, and won third place in the voting for 'Young Player of the Year'.

This enthusiasm for the game and for scoring goals that first attracted Lawrie McMenemy has never left him. 'He has shown this terrific appetite for scoring in every grade of football he's played in,' says Lawrie, who watched him regularly as a youngster and signed him on schoolboy forms at 14.

There was a problem, though, because young Steve, who lived with his widowed mother in a small village near Southampton, was doing well at school. So Lawrie recommended that

he stayed on to take his A-levels, and promised that he could come to the club at 18. This, of course, meant that he missed out on his apprenticeship. 'We had hoped to arrange some sessions for the lad at the club,' said Lawrie, 'but he never seemed to able to fit them in. He was playing for his school, his area, his county, England Schools, and on Sundays!'

When Steve eventually signed for Southampton, having gained his A-levels but turning down a university place, he had a lot to catch up on. 'He had been playing competitive football instead of working at his basic skills,' said Lawrie. 'He still has to learn how to use other people more and to create space for himself and other players.'

A modest and dedicated youngster, Steve is the first to acknowledge how much he owes to the players around him. Although he had made his first-team debut the previous season, coming on as a substitute – and scoring – against Man-

chester City, that had been his only taste of First Division soccer, and he started last season in the reserves. There he might have stayed, at least for another season or two, had it not been for injuries to Kevin Keegan and Charlie George, and then Phil Boyer's departure.

He soon became Southampton's leading scorer, and rose pretty high on the First Division list, too, despite having missed a dozen games. His growing reputation means that he will receive closer attention from the opposition in future. But if he retains his enthusiasm and appetite for scoring, there is no reason why he should not continue to hit the back of the net for many seasons to come.

Lawrie McMenemy, Steve's manager, who first saw him as an enthusiastic 11-year-old slithering around in the mud, is delighted and thrilled with his progress: 'He has shown this terrific appetite for scoring goals in every grade of football he's played in.'

Kevin Keegan, who was not the only Southampton star upstaged by Steve Moran, is generous in his praise: 'Steve's like me in that his game is built on pace and enthusiasm. He's so sharp, and he has that priceless gift for scoring goals.'

The Clough and Taylor Show

For once since Brian Clough and Peter Taylor revived the club's fortunes, Nottingham Forest did not win any major honours. They lost their European title, fell short in domestic competition, and were defeated in the World Club Championship by Nacional of Uruguay.

Nevertheless, the flamboyant pair were rarely out of the headlines, and one could be forgiven for thinking that Nottingham Forest Football Club had been replaced by the 'Clough and Taylor Show'.

The harmonious pair cut a disc 'You Can't Win Them All'. This proved quite prophetic as far as Forest were concerned, but it was a genuine attempt to defuse the violent atmosphere on the terraces of most grounds.

The dauntless 'duo' give their views on the future of soccer at a House of Commons meeting. As Clough relaxes with his shoes off, Taylor looks suitably apprehensive.

This is the nearest they got to the World Club Trophy. Forest made a midweek round trip to Tokyo, where they were unlucky to lose 1-0 to South American champions Nacional.

Quiz Answers

Page 36 WORLD CUP

1. Uruguay beat Argentina 4-2 in the first World Cup final. Argentina are in the lighter shorts, and you can just make out the stripes on the shirt of the player in the foreground (the one with the curious headgear) who has just failed to prevent Uruguay's last goal.
2. The player is Pelé, only 17 but the scorer of two of Brazil's goals. They beat the host country Sweden 5-2 to win their first World Cup.
3. This is the sensational North Korean team after beating Italy 1-0. They qualified for the quarter-finals, where they lost 5-3 to Portugal, but not before frightening the lives out of them with three goals in the first 24 minutes.
4. A shot from England's Geoff Hurst (not in picture) has just rebounded from the cross-bar. After consulting the linesman, the referee gave a goal, and England took the lead in extra time. Hurst eventually scored another, his third, to give England a 4-2 victory over W Germany.
5. It's that man again, Pelé, turning after scoring the first goal in Brazil's 4-1 victory over Italy.
6. The player is Joe Jordan, who is heading the goal that gave Scotland victory over Czechoslovakia and as a result a place in the 1974 finals.
7. Johnny Rep of Holland is heading the ball, which hit a post. Had it gone in, they might have beaten Argentina, who eventually won 3-1 after extra time.

Page 42 EURO-QUIZ

1. The scorer is Alan Sealey. He scored both of West Ham's goals in their 2-0 victory over Munich 1860 at Wembley. (The player in the centre is Martin Peters.)
2. The celebration is at Parkhead, home of Celtic. They had just become the first British side to win the European Cup, and 60,000 fans turned up at the ground to welcome them home in 1967.
3. The players are Nobby Stiles (left) and Bobby Charlton, after Manchester United had beaten Benfica 4-1 in the 1968 European Cup.
4. John Radford is scoring Arsenal's second goal against Anderlecht at Highbury in the second leg of the Fairs Cup final in 1970. They went on to take this leg 3-0 to give them victory 4-3 on aggregate.
5. Francis Lee is scoring from the spot in the final of the 1970 Cup-Winners Cup, in which Manchester City beat Gornik Zabrze of Poland 2-1.
6. Kevin Keegan has just blasted a free-kick through the Bruges wall to score for Liverpool in the second leg of the 1976 UEFA Cup final. Liverpool got a 1-1 draw and won 4-3 on aggregate.
7. Terry McDermott (right) is scoring Liverpool's first goal in their 3-1 European Cup victory over Borussia Mönchengladbach in Rome in 1977.

Page 46 WHAT'S IN A NAME?

1. Ian, of Crystal Palace
2. Mick, of FC Porto
3. Mike, of Bolton Wanderers
4. Paul, of Charlton Athletic
5. Colin, of Notts Forest

Page 51 TRANSFER QUIZ

1. Former England captain Gerry Francis, who went back to his old club Queen's Park Rangers.
2. Martin O'Neill was transferred to Norwich.
3. Craig Johnston of Middlesbrough, who agreed to sign for Liverpool, but not until the season was over.
4. Forest's Ian Bowyer, who signed for Sunderland.
5. Goalkeeper Paul Barron, who came from Arsenal at the same time as Allen.
6. The catch here is that Arsenal were not involved. The player is Norwegian international Jan Einar Aas, who had a trial with Arsenal in October. Nottingham Forest eventually signed him in March from German club Bayern Munich.

Champion Giant Killers

Third Division Exeter reach FA Cup quarter-finals

Lee Roberts (left) grabs a late equaliser up at Newcastle.

No one could have any doubt that Exeter City were the giant-killers of the season. For a middle-of-the-table Third Division side to reach the Sixth Round of the FA Cup has to be a fine achievement. But the style with which Exeter disposed of sides from higher divisions, despite the disadvantage of away draws, won them universal admiration.

Their only home draw was in the First Round, back in November, when they crushed non-League Leatherhead 5-0. Their star striker Tony Kellow scored two. In the Second Round, they beat fellow Division III side Mill-

Three days after beating First Division Leicester 3-1 in a Fourth Round replay, Exeter lost 3-1 at home to Hull, bottom of Division III. So how would you expect bottom-of-Division I Leicester to fare against Liverpool the same day? Well, they won 2-1, and were the first club to win at Anfield for over three years!

wall 1-0 at the Den. In Round 3 they had non-League opposition again, beating Maidstone 4-2. But it was not as easy as the score suggests and they might well have suffered the fate of a Goliath themselves had the ball run a little more kindly for their opponents.

So they were through to Round 4. Drawn away to Leicester, however, they appeared to have little chance, despite Leicester's lowly position in the First Division, especially when they went one down after only five minutes. But Exeter gained in confidence as their loftier opponents faltered, and Kellow made an equaliser for David Pullar in the second half. They outplayed Leicester in the replay, and Kellow notched a hat-trick in the 3-1 victory that took them into the Fifth Round for the first time since 1937.

Exeter's opponents in Round 5 were Second Division Newcastle. In an unexceptional cup-tie, Exeter hung on by sheer doggedness. But they were still trailing to a 57th-minute goal when they produced an unexpected equaliser five minutes from the end. Centre-half Lee Roberts shot in from close range following a long throw.

The replay, however, was all Exeter. In a thrilling exhibition of inspired football, they took the once-mighty Cup-fighters of the North-East to the cleaners. Peter Hatch had an outstanding game, and Ian Pearson scored with a spectacular overhead kick. Three up at

Tony Kellow salutes one of Exeter's four in the replay.

Jubilation as Exeter reach the quarter-finals.

EXETER'S CUP RUN

Round	Opponents		Result
1	L'head	H	5-0
2	Millwall	A	1-0
3	Maidstone	A	4-2
4	Leicester	A	1-1
		H	3-1
5	Newcastle	A	1-1
		H	4-0
6	Spurs	A	0-2

half time, they made it 4-0 just before the end. And so they were in the quarter-finals for only the second time in their history; the first was 50 years earlier.

Had Exeter been favoured with a home draw, who knows what heights they might have risen to in the next round. For the fifth time running, however, they were drawn away, this time to Spurs. They went to White Hart Lane full of hope, and with nothing to lose. But it was not to be. They held out bravely against Ardiles, Archibald, Hoddle, and company for two-thirds of the game, and it was only after they lost Ian Pearson through injury that they finally fell to goals by defenders. Spurs were relieved to get those two goals. They could not have been too happy with their chances had they been forced to replay at Exeter's St James Park.

Villa Pip Ipswich at the Post

As Aston Villa win their first League title for 71 years, West Ham, Rotherham, and Southend take divisional honours

In a thrilling 'two-horse race' for the First Division title, it was not until the last Saturday of the regular season that Aston Villa finally pipped Ipswich at the post to record their seventh Championship win, but their first for 71 years.

Liverpool took up their regular position at the top of the table in December and it was a 2-0 defeat at Villa Park in early January that knocked them off their

Aston Villa celebrate their League Championship triumph in the Highbury dressing-room despite losing to Arsenal on the last Saturday of the season.

How they Finished

Division I

	P	W	D	L	F	A	Pts
Aston Villa	42	26	8	8	72	40	60
Ipswich	42	23	10	9	77	43	56
Arsenal	42	19	15	8	61	45	53
West Bromwich	42	20	12	10	60	42	52

Division II

	P	W	D	L	F	A	Pts
West Ham	42	28	10	4	79	29	66
Notts County	42	18	17	7	49	38	53
Swansea	42	18	14	10	64	44	50
Blackburn	42	16	18	8	42	29	50

Division III

	P	W	D	L	F	A	Pts
Rotherham	46	24	13	9	62	32	61
Barnsley	46	21	17	8	72	45	59
Charlton	46	25	9	12	63	44	59
Huddersfield	46	21	14	11	71	40	56

Division IV

	P	W	D	L	F	A	Pts
Southend	46	30	7	9	79	31	67
Lincoln	46	25	15	6	66	25	65
Doncaster	46	22	12	12	59	49	56
Wimbledon	46	23	9	14	64	46	55

perch. They clung on tenaciously for a couple of months, but they finally left the stage to Villa and Ipswich.

Of the two, Ipswich were favourites, taking over the No. 1 spot immediately and holding it until the beginning of April. They were in the running for a remarkable treble — League, Cup, and UEFA Cup. They were playing some of the finest football in the country. But then they were desperately unlucky with injuries, losing Burley and Beattie for the season and other stars for important matches. Yet they kept coming back. Only four days after defeat in the semi-finals of the FA Cup, they won 2-1 at Villa Park to get within a point of the leaders. But they 'blew it' at their own Portman Road the following Saturday when Arsenal destroyed their 46-game unbeaten home run with a 2-0 victory and virtually put paid to their Championship chances.

The last Saturday arrived, though, with Ipswich needing to win at Middlesbrough and then at home to Southampton, while Villa had to lose at Highbury to Arsenal. And it was Arsenal, coming with a late surge themselves for a place in the following season's UEFA Cup, who gave Ipswich their last chance. At half-time they led Villa 2-0 and Ipswich were a goal up at Ayresome Park. But it was not to be. Middlesbrough scored twice, and although Villa could make no impression on Arsenal, their 16,000 fans at Highbury turned their attentions to their transistor radios and suddenly went wild as the news of Middlesbrough's goals came through. It was a curious spectacle at Highbury, in front of the season's highest gate (57,472), with both sets of fans celebrating, the winners for gaining a place in Europe and the losers for gaining the League crown!

The last Saturday of the season saw several other important issues settled, not least the battle for promotion from Division II. West Ham had sewn up the Second Division title long before, though. Taking the lead for the second time in mid-November, they never relinquished it, gradually opening up an enormous gap between themselves

and an ever-changing group of hopefuls whose collective motto seemed to be 'After you'. While West Ham were giving regular displays of class football that any First Division side would have been proud of, their rivals were notable only for their apparent reluctance to accept one of the other promotion spots.

The most remarkable decline was Chelsea's. Second in the table half-way through the season and playing some fine attacking football, they suddenly lost the art of scoring goals. They scored only two in their last 13 matches! Notts County won promotion with only 49 goals, four fewer than the 53 points that gave them second place.

Goalscoring, on average, was abysmally low in the

Second Division. Blackburn, who finished fourth, scored only 42 – one a game – and Grimsby, who were in contention until the last week, finished up with a 44–42 goal record. Even more astonishing, perhaps, was Newcastle's 11th place with only 30 goals.

The final promotion spot was clinched on the last Saturday by John Toshack's Swansea City. Second in January, the 'Swans' suf-

A symbolic illustration of Second Division fortunes as West Ham's Alan Devonshire leaps over Chelsea's Graham Wilkins. West Ham won this early clash at Stamford Bridge 1-0, thanks to an own goal by the unfortunate Wilkins. They soon went to the top of the table and won the championship by 13 clear points, while Chelsea finished well down.

61

The Third Division proved an unhappy resting place for two of England's 1966 World Cup heroes, Martin Peters and Alan Ball, player-managers of Sheffield United and Blackpool, respectively. Peters (above, firing a free-kick at the Charlton wall) took over during the season as manager of United, who at one time in September were top of the table. But they plummeted right down and were relegated in their last match. Blackpool knew their fate earlier, but by then Ball had lost his job and found himself back in the First Division again, playing for Southampton (below, with Gary Shaw of Aston Villa).

fered a disastrous spell that plummeted them to 11th before a fine recovery in April won them a place in Division I for the first time in their history. Only six years previously, they had found themselves applying for re-election to the Fourth Division. Then Toshack arrived as player-manager and took them to the First in a record four years. Their late revival was due largely to recovery from injury and return to form of international winger Leighton James.

The Third Division also produced its share of promotion 'jitters'. Charlton Athletic, who had led the table for most of the season until the end of March, and had appeared certainties for promotion, suddenly found themselves struggling. They eventually scraped through in third place, thanks largely to the failings of others. Entering the last lap at the beginning of April, they had a four-point lead, but they could scramble only five points in their last seven games.

Rotherham, who finished two points ahead of Barnsley and Charlton, owed their success to an unbeaten home record and steady away form — and, of course, to the ability and drive of their manager Ian Porterfield. Scorer of Sunderland's winning goal against Leeds in the 1973 Cup final, Porterfield worked his magic on Rotherham in less than two seasons.

In the Fourth Division, Southend took over at the top from Lincoln City in mid-October and the two teams remained in first and second place, respectively, for the rest of the season. Winning 19 home games and drawing the remainder, Southend amassed 67 points in all. They conceded only six goals on their own ground.

There was quite a scramble mid-season for the other promotion places, but Wimbledon clinched one of them and Doncaster edged them into fourth place.

Many of the League's relegation issues were not settled until the closing stages of the season. One exception, however, was Crystal Palace, who found themselves in the last three in early September and never managed to get out of the rut. With three changes of manager, numerous transfers, and one takeover, the club drifted from crisis to crisis. They finished 13 points adrift at the bottom, and were the only club in the League who failed to win an away match. They were joined in the drop by Leicester, whose young side had played some good football and had in the process earned the singular honour of ending Liverpool's remarkable three-year unbeaten home record. They also ended Norwich's hopes of First Division survival by defeating them 3-2 at Carrow Road on the last Saturday of the season.

It was a sad season for Bristol, both sides suffering relegation. Rovers took over bottom position from City in mid-October and stayed there, and City never emerged from the relegation zone. The battle to avoid being the third doomed club developed into a straight fight between Cardiff and Preston. Fellow Welsh side

Liverpool's **Terry McDermott (right) watches Leicester striker Jim Melrose on the attack in an early-season match at Filbert Street. It was sad to see Leicester's promising young side go down at the end of the season, but they had the consolation not only of this 2-0 home win over the Champions, but in the return in January of becoming the first side to win at Anfield for over three years.**

Swansea did Cardiff a good turn by beating Preston at Deepdale on the last Saturday of the season. But it was not until the following Wednesday that Cardiff made themselves safe by holding champions West Ham at home. Proud Preston, despite a gallant away victory over Derby, found themselves relegated on goal difference.

In the Third Division, Walsall saved themselves from the drop with a last-ditch effort, a 1-0 away win over Sheffield United. This had the effect of sending United down, and the Sheffield club suffered the rare mortification of being relegated with a 'plus' goal difference, scoring 65 goals and conceding 63. Going down with them were Colchester, Blackpool and Hull.

There were a record number of managerial casualties during the season, including Blackpool's player-manager Alan Ball, who himself finished up again in the First Division – playing for Southampton. It was a disastrous season, too, for all the other managers who had been English World Cup heroes in 1966. Geoff Hurst lost his job at Chelsea, Nobby Stiles (Preston) and Martin Peters (Sheffield United) both suffered relegation – and soon after, lost their jobs – while Jackie Charlton's hopes of taking Sheffield Wednesday up to the First Division were thwarted by their inability to reproduce their home form away from Hillsborough.

But the sorriest managerial dismissal was that of Dave Sexton from Manchester United. Constantly attacked by a section of the northern Press who found him uncommunicative, Sexton managed to keep United in a mid-table position despite mounting injuries to key players. The fans, however, brought up on a 'diet' of Best, Law, and Bobby Charlton, and 'brainwashed' by adverse Press reports, clamoured for his head. Unaccountably swayed by this pressure, the United board sacked Sexton at the end of the season – a season in which they had finished a respectable eighth and won their last seven matches!

The Scottish Season

The 'Auld Firm' back on top

Celtic regained the League title they had relinquished in 1980 to Aberdeen. Not that the Dons gave it up without a fight. Their early season form promised to build on their 1980 success, but Celtic caught them in the New Year and gradually pulled away until they finished seven points clear. Their 56 points, 26 wins, and 84 goals were all records for the six-year-old Premier Division.

Things had looked different back in December, when, two days after Christmas, the Dons thrashed them 4-1 at Pittodrie to open up a three-point lead at the top with a game in hand. But manager Billy McNeill had a 'quiet word' with the players after this setback, and in the next 14 games Celtic picked up 27 points out of a possible 28, an irresistible burst of form.

McNeill could be well satisfied with the season, not only for the superb football they played but also for his success in introducing a number of youngsters into the side. The most spectacular was the high-scoring Charlie Nicholas up front, but Pat Bonner, who replaced the injured Peter Latchford in goal, was just as valuable. Another huge success was the previous season's acquisition from Liverpool, striker Frank McGarvey, who was the League's leading scorer with

23 goals. Other youngsters to 'come of age' in Celtic's season were Mark Reid and John Weir. With Murdo McLeod rediscovering his scoring touch after injury, Danny McGrain still an inspiring captain at the back, the skills of Dave Provan and new cap Tommy Burns in midfield, watch out for Glasgow Celtic in Europe next season!

Celtic, however, did not have it all their own way in Scotland. It isn't for nothing that Dundee United are called 'The Terrors', and they toppled Celtic in the semi-finals of both the League Cup and the Scottish FA Cup.

The League Cup final was a strangely domestic affair – played at Dundee's Dens Park between Dundee and Dundee United, with a Dundee referee in charge. In the event, United retained the trophy with an easy 3-0 victory, the goals coming from David Dodds and Paul Sturrock (two).

Although they did not win the Cup, United's performance in the semi-finals was outstanding. Twice they outplayed Celtic, being held to a goalless draw the first time largely owing to a brilliant display by Bonner in the Celtic goal, but overcoming the eventual champions in the replay by three goals to two. Paul Heggarty was an inspiring captain for United and the talents of Dave

Narey and Eamonn Bannon were always evident. But the man who stole the headlines was manager Jim McLean – 'Mr Perfection'. After they thrashed Motherwell 6-1 in the quarter-finals, he 'fined' the players £20 each, or so it was said. In fact, he docked the £20 off their maximum £60 'entertainment bonus', and the players agreed with the decision!

McLean couldn't have been too happy with his team's performance in the final against Rangers, however. They outplayed the 'Blues' in the first match, but their failure to finish cost them victory. Indeed, Rangers would have won it but for missing a penalty with the last kick of normal time. The culprit was Ian Redford, whose weak spot-kick was saved by Hamish McAlpine. It was Rangers keeper, Jim Stewart, though, who deserved most of the credit for keeping the scoresheet goalless. The replay was a different story, and Rangers thrashed United 4-1.

Rangers had a curious season, finishing a distant third in the League. Thanks to Redford's penalty miss, though, they were given a final chance to shine, and in the replay they turned in their finest performance of the season. Manager John Greig at last achieved the right attacking blend, the young Redford retrieved his name with a confident display, and John MacDonald finished off two fine moves to clinch the game for Rangers.

So the 'Auld Firm' of Celtic and Rangers once again shared Scotland's major trophies.

Hibs ran away with the First Division, five points in front of Dundee, who leapfrogged into a promotion place over St Johnstone with a 1-0 away win (over East Stirling) on the last day of the season. Stirling and Berwick were well and truly relegated.

Their places were taken by the two 'Queens'. On the last day of the season, Queen's Park, already sure of the Division II title, did Queen of the South a good turn by winning at Cowdenbeath. This enabled Queen of the South to overtake 'Beath with an easy 3-0 home win over lowly Albion Rovers.

But the last word must go to Arbroath, whose last-day defeat of Stenhousemuir was only their third League home win of the season, fewer than any other side in Division II. Their total of 10 away wins, however, was the highest in the division!

How they Finished

Premier Division

	P	W	D	L	F	A	Pts
Celtic	36	26	4	6	84	37	56
Aberdeen	36	19	11	6	61	26	49
Rangers	36	16	12	8	60	32	44

Division I

	P	W	D	L	F	A	Pts
Hibernian	39	24	9	6	67	24	57
Dundee	39	22	8	9	64	40	52
St Johnstone	39	20	11	8	64	45	51

Division II

	P	W	D	L	F	A	Pts
Queen's Park	39	16	18	5	62	43	50
Queen of the South	39	16	14	9	66	53	46
Cowdenbeath	39	18	9	12	63	48	45

Partick Thistle's Alan Rough was voted Scotland's Footballer of the Year. He still continued to make costly mistakes in internationals, however, and St Mirren's Billy Thomson emerged as a rival for the Scottish goalkeeping jersey.

Home International Championship

Is this the end of football's oldest international competition?

The Home International Championship was born way back in the 1883–84 season and is soccer's oldest international series. But for many years, now, it has been declining in importance and popularity, and the events of 1981 left serious doubts as to whether it would survive to celebrate its centenary in 1983–84.

Since 1969, the Championship has been staged in eight days at the end of the season. Last season, however, it was decided to discontinue this practice. For the 1981–82 season, half the fixtures were scheduled for midweek dates in February and April, with the rest to be played at the end of the season, but only the England–Scotland fixture on a Saturday.

It was the England–Scotland fixture that hit the headlines earlier, when the Football Association announced that there would be no allocation or sale of tickets for the Wembley match 'north of the border'. This was an effort to eliminate the hooliganism and drunkenness associated with the traditional 'tartan invasion' of London for the game. The FA threatened to scrap the fixture altogether if there was a repeat of the vandalism of recent years.

Anyone churlish enough to suggest that the FA perhaps were losing interest in

Leighton James (right) and Ray Stewart clash at Swansea. James entertained his home crowd with a delightful display of old-fashioned wing play, while West Ham's Stewart made an encouraging debut.

the Home Championship had fuel added to their fire when the FA suddenly withdrew from the game with Northern Ireland at only four days' notice. Admittedly the situation in Belfast was worrying because of the increasing violence connected with the IRA hunger strike, but the FA could have foreseen this weeks before. The decision – made without consulting the Irish FA or the players themselves – showed a marked lack of consideration, for it did not even allow time for the fixture to be rearranged and played in England.

The Welsh then pulled out of their fixture in Belfast,

having first consulted their players. So the Championship became quite meaningless, the remaining games being used as practice matches for the World Cup squads.

The 'competition' finally began in Swansea on 16 May, when Wales proceeded to wipe the floor with a largely experimental Scottish team lacking strikers Dalglish, Archibald, and Andy Gray. What football there was was all played by Wales. But it is difficult not to be cynical about a game in which both goals were 'gifted' by Scottish Footballer of the Year Alan Rough's inability to handle crosses. Scotland's only memorable piece of action all day was an off-the-ball incident which resulted in their striker Joe Jordan being sent off. Fortunately, only 18,985 people turned up to watch the game.

There were few more at Hampden Park the following Tuesday to see Scotland take on the defending champions Northern Ireland. As it was their only match, the Irish were hardly in a position to defend only the second outright title they had won in their history, and it is not surprising that they went down 2–0 to a Scottish side showing seven changes from the one defeated by Wales.

One bright spot for manager Jock Stein was the form and versatility of West Ham's Ray Stewart. Having made his international debut against Wales as both right-back and left-back (moving across at half-time), he now had a midfield role. And he scored a cracking goal after five minutes, collecting a square free-kick 22 yards out and hammering the ball low past Jennings. The other goal, scored in the second half, was also a gem to cheer the scattered fans on Hampden's crumbling terraces. Asa Hartford hit a perfect long through-ball into the path of Steve Archibald on the left. The Spurs striker, fresh from their FA Cup victory the previous week, took it in his stride and slid the ball into the opposite corner of the goal.

The less said about England's goalless draw with Wales the better. England were going through their worst ever spell at Wembley, and this was their fourth successive game without a win; their third without scoring. They extended these unwelcome records further a few days later when they lost 1−0 to Scotland in the final match of the Championship.

The FA's plan to keep out the invading hordes of Scottish fans came to nothing, as upwards of 50,000 somehow managed to acquire tickets. As a result, this traditional clash became virtually a home match for the Scots who outnumbered the English supporters by nearly two to one in the 90,000 crowd.

The match itself was a scrappy affair, but the tremendous atmosphere

John Robertson (right) sends Corrigan the wrong way from the spot, and that goal was enough to give Scotland their victory at Wembley.

created by the opposing sets of fans inspired the players to all-out effort. The most colourful character on the field was French referee Robert Wurtz, but he would have been more at home in a circus. He rightly gave Scotland a penalty in the 65th minute when Bryan Robson pulled Archibald down after he had been put clear by Provan. Forest's John Robertson, having a fine game, sent Corrigan the wrong way from the spot-kick. But the referee inexplicably failed to award England a penalty when Willie Miller, the inspiration of Scotland's defence, blatantly held Trevor Francis back as he was going past him. England had far more of the play, but squandered the chances they managed to create, and Scotland battled bravely after losing Hartford early on.

The Scottish fans went home happy and without leaving their customary trail of destruction. FA Secretary Ted Croker said that England would be at Hampden next year. (Whether Hampden would be there was another matter, depending perhaps on the miraculous appear-

ance of a millionaire benefactor willing to foot the bill to restore that grand old ground.) It seemed that the England–Scotland fixture was safe for the time being, but the fate of the Championship was in the balance.

Who won the Home International Championship? Well, the respective FAs promised to get together some time to sort it out, but your guess is as good as theirs. The 'table' finished up like this:

	P	W	D	L	F	A	Pts	%
Scotland	3	2	0	1	3	2	4	67
Wales	2	1	1	0	2	0	3	75
England	2	0	1	1	0	1	1	25
N.Ireland	1	0	0	1	0	2	0	0

So Scotland 'won' on points, and Wales finished top on percentage points. But we could always call it 'no contest', in which case Northern Ireland are still champions. They deserve to be after the way they were treated.

What of the future? It is obvious that with today's congested domestic programme and the comprehensive European and world competition, there is no longer a place for the Home International Championship. Yet it would be a shame for football if, through the greed of the stronger soccer countries, we were to lose this historic and traditional 'friendly' competition.

English Clubs Dominate Europe

Liverpool and Ipswich show England how it's done

While England were struggling to win a place in the World Cup finals, her top teams were running away with the honours at club level. Liverpool triumphed in the European Cup for the third time. Following Nottingham Forest's double, it was the fifth successive win for an English club. And Ipswich won the UEFA Cup, their first taste of European success.

With holders for the past two years Forest crashing out in the First Round to CSKA Sofia, losing both ties 1-0, it was up to Liverpool to maintain England's remarkable recent record in the European Cup. Liverpool had not had the brightest of starts themselves, held 1-1 in Finland by Oulun Palloseura. At Anfield, however, they smashed the Finns 10-1, with hat-tricks by Souness and McDermott.

In the Second Round they faced Aberdeen, who had scraped through on a 1-0 aggregate over Austria Vienna. McDermott finished off a superb movement with a cheeky chip over the keeper at Pittodrie to give Liverpool a 1-0 first-leg lead. And at Anfield they gave the stylish Scottish champions a lesson in football with a masterly 4-0 win.

They met Forest's conquerors CSKA in the quarter-finals, and in one of the finest exhibitions of the

The European Cup final was a game of few chances. A perfect sliding tackle from Real Madrid's Uli Stielike denies Liverpool's David Johnson one (above). It was a defender, Alan Kennedy (right), who finally broke through, despite an injured wrist.

season crushed them 5-1 at Anfield aided by another Souness hat-trick — all cracking goals. The return was a formality, and Liverpool took it 1-0.

The semi-finals were probably Liverpool's greatest test. At Anfield, with Souness and Johnson missing and McDermott substituted through injury, they were held to a goalless draw by a Bayern Munich side marshalled by Paul Breitner and inspired by the dangerous raiding of Karl-Heinz Rummenigge, European Footballer of the Year. And they were really up against it in

the return, this time without Thompson and Alan Kennedy, when Dalglish was crudely brought down after two minutes and had to be substituted. In their 113th match in European competition, however, Liverpool exhibited all the assurance of true champions, and their experience saw them through. In the 83rd minute, the limping Johnson picked up a long clearance from Clemence and crossed it to captain-for-the-night Ray Kennedy, who coolly chested the ball down and rifled it past the keeper. Although Rummenigge scored in the last three minutes, Liverpool deservedly held out to win on the away goals rule.

Liverpool's opponents in the final in Paris were six-times champions Real Madrid. The Spaniards had conceded only three goals in reaching the final, two of them to little Limerick in the First Round. They had Uli Stielike, the West German star, in midfield, and two marvellous ball-players in Juanito and England winger Laurie Cunningham, back after a long injury.

In the pattern of recent European Cup finals, it was no classic and was settled by a single goal, after 81 minutes. Liverpool who were back to full strength at last, had done most of the pressing in a game with few clear-cut openings. Then, Ray Kennedy took a throw-in on the left, near the Real goal line. There seemed little danger when Alan Kennedy chested it down into the 'box', but Garcia Cortes took a wild swing at the ball and Kennedy brushed past him, took the ball on and from a narrow angle joyfully slammed it left-footed past the keeper.

Unlike the Champions Cup, the two-legged UEFA Cup final was full of goals and incidents and near misses. This was not surprising, because both Ipswich and AZ 67 Alkmaar had scored freely on their way to the final.

In the early rounds, Ipswich reminded their travelling fans of their failing in previous European campaigns — a tendency to col-

Ipswich manager Bobby Robson proudly displays the UEFA Cup, after a sparkling two-legged final with Dutch side AZ.

lapse in the away leg. In Salonika they almost lost their 5-1 home advantage (Wark had scored four of them) when Aris went 3-0 up in 65 minutes, but a Gates goal made them safe. Then, in Prague, Bohemians cut their 3-0 deficit to one in 54 minutes. Again, Ipswich held out. In the Third Round, a Wark hat-trick helped Ipswich to an unassailable 5-0 home leg against Widzew Lodz, the Polish conquerors of Manchester United.

The quarter-finals saw Ipswich produce the sensation of the season. They went to France and beat St-Etienne 4-1 despite an early Johnny Rep goal that took the home side's goal tally in the competition to 23-0! A confident 3-1 win in the return ensured Ipswich's place in the semi-finals, where they enjoyed two dour 1-0 victories over Cologne.

AZ were the new Dutch champions, and had scored 29 goals so far in the UEFA Cup. But at Portman Road, Ipswich made them look ordinary and built up a 3-0 lead. When AZ threw caution to the winds in the last few minutes, they made and missed two good chances, but it was a warning to Ipswich for the return.

A superb 20-yard volley from one of their own Dutch stars, Frans Thijssen, in four minutes gave Ipswich a dream start and meant that AZ had to score at least five. With their skilful sweeper Metgod permanently in attack, AZ threw everything at Ipswich and scored twice. But then John Wark scored an important goal. It not only virtually assured Ipswich of the trophy, but equalled the 14-goal record for a season of European competition set by Jose Altafini when AC Milan won the European Cup in 1963. Even so, AZ refused to surrender. Playing some of the finest attacking football seen all season, they scored twice more. But Ipswich thoroughly deserved their 5-4 aggregate victory.

There were other notable performances by British sides in Europe, including Dundee United's 7-2 thrashing of Polish side Slask Wroclaw at Tannadice Park in the UEFA Cup. The last word, though, must go to lowly Newport County who were within a whisker of becoming the first ever Third Division club to reach a European semi-final. But they were beaten 1-0 at home by Carl Zeiss Jena in what was surely the unluckiest match of the season, when a draw would have seen them through.

Top: Red and yellow cards were discontinued by the Football League during the season. One player to 'see red' before the new ruling was Wednesday's Terry Curran, and his dismissal unfortunately led to a serious crowd disturbance.

Centre: Manager John Lyall and Trevor Brooking enjoy a West Ham training session.

Bottom: Olympic gold-medallist Sebastian Coe visits the England team during training, and poses with Graham Rix (left) and Eric Gates.